baby einstein®

Numbers

The WALT DISNEY Company

Hyperion Books for Children, New York
Copyright © 2004 by The Baby Einstein Company, LLC.
All Rights Reserved.
Baby Einstein and the Boy's Head Logo are trademarks of The Baby Einstein Company, LLC. All Rights Reserved.
EINSTEIN and ALBERT EINSTEIN are trademarks of The Hebrew University of Jerusalem. All Rights Reserved.
For information address Hyperion Books for Children, 114 Fifth Avenue, New York, New York 10011-5690.
Printed in China
Library of Congress Cataloging Card Number on file.
ISBN 0-7868-3805-1

Visit www.hyperionbooksforchildren.com and www.babyeinstein.com

Great Minds Start Little.™

Let's Count

one

1

one baby

Let's Count

two
1 2

two drums

three
1 2 3

three dolls

Let's Count

four

1 2 3 4

four flowers

Let's Count

five

1 2 3 4 5

five teddy bears

See and Spy Counting

How many barns do you see?

How many ears does the cow have?

How many bells are around the cow's neck?

How many blades of grass are in the cow's mouth?

How many spots can you count on the cow?

See and Spy Counting

How many red tongues are in the dog's mouth?

How many eyes does the dog have?

How many bees are flying by?

How many flowers is the dog peeking through?

How many pads are on the dog's paw?

See and Spy Counting

How many suns do you see?

How many puffy clouds are in the sky?

How many butterflies are in the air?

How many paws does the tiger have?

How many black stripes are on the tiger's back?

See and Spy Counting

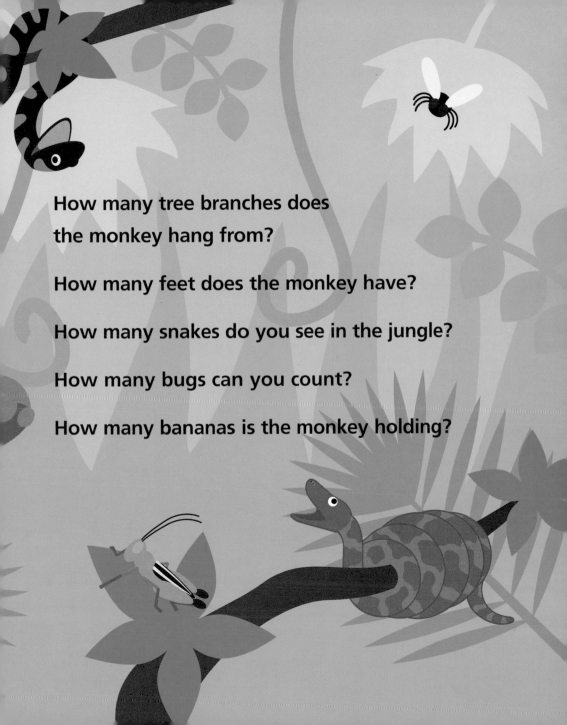

How many tree branches does
the monkey hang from?

How many feet does the monkey have?

How many snakes do you see in the jungle?

How many bugs can you count?

How many bananas is the monkey holding?

See and Spy Counting

How many beaks are on the penguin?

How many flippers does the penguin have?

How many snowmen do you see?

How many fish did the penguin catch for dinner?

How many snowflakes can you count?